PA

GW00394316

The Man an

STUDIES IN THE
ACTS OF THE APOSTLES

David Greenaway

GROUP BIBLE STUDY SERIES

LEADER'S BOOK

MOORLEY'S Print & Publishing

ISBN 0 86071 411 X

MOORLEY'S Print & Publishing
23 Park Road, Ilkeston, Derbys, DE7 5DA - England.

PREFACE

These studies are about Mission. The essential task of the Church is Mission to all people, with no discrimination. The purpose of the Church is to bear witness to Jesus.

The six topics are:

An introduction to the Acts of the Apostles and to Paul (Saul).

Paul's conversion and calling.

Paul's first missionary journey.

Paul's second missionary journey.

Paul's third missionary journey.

Paul's arrest and imprisonment.

This Book complements the Personal Preparation Studies. The aim of the material is to equip and encourage the leader of a small study group to steer the meeting on its course.

PREPARATION NOTES FOR LEADERS OF SMALL STUDY GROUPS

The Aims of the Group Leader

To be a guide to the group NOT a teacher.

To keep the group moving so that all the material is covered within the time.

To play referee in discussion and keep it from straying too far from the subject.

To ask the questions provided and to let the group answer them.

The idea of the study group outline is that the groups do the work and the leader simply steers it on course.

Encourage the group to bring their own Bible together with their Personal Preparation Study Book.

Home Work. Before you go to take a group:

1. Read these Guidelines for Leaders of Small Study Groups.
2. Note and prepare any special requirements.
3. Use the Personal Preparation Studies.
4. Pray for yourself and one member of your group each day.

Advice

1. Don't spend all the group time on one question.
2. If you have a question, ask your minister.
3. If you have a problem with your group, share it with your minister.
4. If you can't lead one week, make a firm arrangement with someone else to take your place.

PRAYERS

1. Begin and close with prayer yourself.
2. Don't ask people to open or close in prayer without asking them beforehand.
   Never drop on people out of the blue to pray.
3. Don't pray round in a prayer chain.

PRAYER TIME AT THE END

Some groups may like to join in a time of open prayer. This will be up to the group leader's discretion as each group may be different. Close each prayer time yourself, and don't let it go on too long.

BIBLE READING

1. Don't ask people to read aloud without warning.
2. Don't read round the group.

3. Ask for volunteers, if no one offers read it yourself.
4. If you ask people:
   a) wait till you know them.
   b) give them a chance to look at it BEFORE they come.
   c) give them a chance to say no.
5. Take spare Bibles.
6. If there are those in your group who don't know their Bibles, give guidance on where to find each passage.
7. For a change you might let the group read silently to themselves.
8. If someone likes reading, use them but don't overdo it.

DISCUSSION
1. Read the questions, let the group find the answers.
2. Don't be afraid of silence.
3. Don't answer questions yourself. SUGGEST possible answers but only do this if they are really stuck.
4. Don't talk too much yourself.
5. Keep the discussion on the subject.
6. Only ask for comment from quiet members when you know them and they have settled into the group.
7. If one member dominates discussion, ask them not to answer the next question so others can share in the discussion, OR ask for comment from those who have not spoken yet. If all else fails have a discreet word with them on their own.

Tea/Coffee
At the close of each group meeting your host/hostess may wish to serve a cup of tea or coffee.

GROUP LEADER'S GUIDELINE

ONE

An introduction to the Acts of the Apostles and to Paul (Saul)

1. READ Acts 2: 41-47.
   Now discuss the life and worship of the Church as seen in this Scripture portion.
   Seek to draw from the group the importance of TEACHING RECEIVED THROUGH GOD'S WORD ("learning from the Apostles"), FELLOWSHIP, SHARING IN THE COMMUNION (this was a major part of their "fellowship meals"), PRAYER.
   The Early Church saw many miracles and wonders. Do we expect God to act in this way through His Church today?
   They shared their possessions with one another and distributed their money among all, according to their need. How can we do this today?

2. READ Acts 1: 8
   The Church is called to Mission. The task is not yet completed! How can we be involved in Christ's Mission within our community? Remember it will not be easy. We are in a battle. We have an enemy. Satan is seen everywhere, operating to hinder and spoil the work of God.

3. READ Acts 8: 3 and 9: 1-2.
   Paul (Saul) demonstrated his religious zeal by persecuting the Christian Church. It is possible to be religious but not a true Christian. We should expect opposition from such people within the Church today.

Close with prayer.

* Use additional material from the Preparation Study as necessary OR use studies one and two in one meeting.

TWO
Paul's conversion and calling.

1. READ Acts 9: 3-9
   It could be helpful if a few members of the group could share their personal experience of Conversion. Try to encourage them to share something of their life <u>before</u> they met Jesus, <u>how</u> they met Jesus and <u>after/since</u> they met Jesus.

   You may find it necessary to take the group through the section in the Personal Preparation Study headed: What is Conversion? Explaining the statement taken from "A Catechism for the use of the people called Methodists".

2. READ Acts 9: 10-20.
   As God called Ananias and Paul to serve Him, so He calls us today. He wants to use us for His glory and the blessing of others. Now spend some moments in an attitude of quietness and prayer to enable the group to consider their response to God's call.

   NOW READ 1 Timothy 1: 12-17.

A Closing Prayer:

> 'Lord, we thank You for the personal joy there is to be found in receiving You as our Saviour and Lord. We leave with You all those who are unsure about this, and those too who are blind to their own need of You. Bring them to faith and personal assurance that they are truly Your children through receiving Christ into their lives. Amen.'

*　Use additional material from the Preparation Study as necessary <u>OR</u> use studies one and two in one meeting.

GROUP LEADER'S GUIDELINE

THREE

Paul's first missionary journey

(Recorded in Acts 13: 1-14: 28)

Introduction: You may wish to allow a few opening minutes for members of the group to talk in general about Paul's first missionary journey. The length of the journey. The difficult sea crossings. The rough overland terrain. The bandit-infested areas. The heat and the cold etc.

1. READ Acts 13: 1-3.
   Barnabas and Saul (Paul) were <u>appointed as missionaries at a Church meeting under the guidance of the Holy Spirit</u>. They were <u>commissioned by the Church.</u> What does this say to the Church today about appointments to the work of the Church through ministry and mission?

2. READ Acts 13: 5, 14 and 14:1. AND Acts 13: 46-49.
   Paul had a strategy for Mission:
   a) He targetted the Synagogues to provide an important and necessary nucleus of converts for the early local Churches.
   b) He went to the strategic centres of communication to establish centres of witness.
   c) He took the Good News to those who were receptive to the message. How can we apply these principles through our Mission activities within our community?

3. READ Acts 13: 8-11.
   Paul confronted opposition. He understood the importance of engaging in Spiritual Warfare.
   We will face opposition today. How can we engage in spiritual warfare?

4. READ Acts 14: 27-28.
   Paul recognised the need to maintain responsible links with the sending Church in Syrian Antioch.
   We cannot work for God in isolation. We need the practical support and prayers of our Church surrounding us in our work for the Lord.
   GOD DOES NOT CALL US TO BECOME HIS 'LONE RANGER'!

5. READ Acts 13: 16-33 AND 14: 14-18.
   Take the group through the section in the Personal Preparation Study headed: Paul's Message. Are we faithful in our sharing of the Christian

Message, from the pulpit, in our weekly activities, through our personal faith sharing?

6. READ Acts 15: 7-11.
    The first Church Council of the Early Church was called to discuss the struggle of Christianity with Judaism (The Narrow isolationism of the Hebrew faith). Do we struggle over a similar issue today with Christianity and narrow traditionalism?

A CLOSING CHALLENGE:

Our Church is the means by which others within our community may come to know the Lord!

Close with Prayer.

GROUP LEADER'S GUIDELINE
FOUR
Paul's second missionary journey

(Recorded in Acts 15: 36-18: 22)

1. READ Acts 15: 36-41.

A difference arose between Barnabas and Paul over the question of whether Mark should accompany them. The two decided to separate and the result of this separation was that two missionary expeditions, rather than one, set out.

In our work with the Lord we will sometimes experience misunderstandings and disagreements with others. We must learn to accept our differences of understanding and remain faithful to our calling by God - His work must continue!

2. READ Acts 16: 6-10.

Under the Holy Spirit's direction the journey becomes a full-scale missionary campaign that took them out of Asia Minor and into Macedonia and Greece - THE GOSPEL ENTERED OUR OWN CONTINENT OF EUROPE!

What does this say to us about our work for the Lord in ministry and Mission? - Are we open to the Holy Spirit's directing?

3. READ Acts 16: 14-15.

Now take the group through the outline steps in Lydia's Conversion from the Personal Preparation Study.

1. She was a religious worshipper of God.
2. She heard Paul's message and the Lord opened her mind to receive His Word.
3. She gave outward expression of her salvation.

Try to encourage some members of the group to share their experience of conversion (testimony).

Other members of the group may find it helpful to ask them questions about their conversion.

4. READ Acts 16: 27-34.

Following the above testimony and question time some members of the group may be inwardly asking the same question as the Philippian Jailer: "What must I do to be saved?"

Now take the group through the answer given by Paul and Silas: "Believe in the Lord Jesus, and you will be saved" - This one short statement shows the necessity of trust in, and commitment to Jesus Christ as Saviour, Lord and Friend.

* The aim of this group meeting is to see people "filled with joy, because they now believe in the Lord". (The experience of the Jailer and his family).

5. READ Acts 17: 22-34.

Now ask the group to silently think through their response to God's Word -In closing read aloud the Challenge:
What is your response to God's Good News concerning our Lord Jesus Christ?

Close with Prayer.

GROUP LEADER'S GUIDELINE
FIVE

Paul's third missionary journey

(Recorded in Acts 18: 23-21:16)

Introduction: You could open this group discussion by considering the four major aspects of ministry and mission seen to be operating on this third missionary journey:

Strengthening the Believers
Teaching on the Holy Spirit
Preaching the Kingdom of God.
Performing great miracles.

Are these aspects of the Church's ministry and mission important to us today?

How can we put them into operation through the life of our Church?

1. READ Acts 19: 20.

   Do we have an expectancy to see the Word of the Lord spreading and growing in a powerful way through our Ministry and Mission?

2. READ Acts 20: 17-38
   Now discuss Paul's farewell speech to the Elders of the Church in Ephesus.
   Those of us in positions of leadership should take heed to God's Word to us in verses 28-31.

Close with Prayer.

* You could include a Bible Study covering Paul's stay of 27 months in Ephesus, recorded in Acts 19: 1-20: 1. <u>OR</u> use Studies Five and Six in one meeting.

GROUP LEADER'S GUIDELINE

SIX

Paul's arrest and imprisonment

(Recorded in Acts 21: 27-28: 31)

1. READ Acts 21: 37-22: 21.

   In this final quarter of the Book Luke is concerned to present Paul as A WITNESS ON TRIAL FOR THE GOSPEL. Paul in his defence acts as a witness of Jesus Christ. He gives a clear testimony to his conversion and to his call to preach to the Gentiles.

   Do we have a story to tell of what God has done, and is still doing, in and through our lives?

2. In Acts 27 we have the dramatic record of the storm at sea and the resulting shipwreck. Through the storm and the shipwreck Paul's trust in God is clearly presented.

   In difficult situations and testing circumstances, is our trust in God clearly presented?

   Always remember - God is in control. He is our protector.

3. READ Acts 28: 17-24.

   The non-Christian Jews spent a full day listening to Paul explaining his message concerning the Kingdom of God and he tried to convince them about Jesus. Some were convinced, but others would not believe.

   A PERSONAL CHALLENGE - Are you convinced about Jesus? Have you made a full commitment of your whole life to Christ?

4. NOW CLOSE THIS FINAL STUDY BY TURNING BACK TO ACTS CHAPTER 1 VERSE 8 and prayerfully reading the words as a closing challenge.

   God is calling us today to be powerful witnesses of our Lord - THE TASK OF MISSION IS NOT YET COMPLETED!

Close with Prayer.

* Use additional material from the Preparation Study as necessary OR use Studies Five and Six in one meeting.

NOTES

MOORLEY'S

are growing Publishers, adding several new titles to our list each year. We also undertake private publications and commissioned works.

Our range of publications includes: **Books of Verse**
Devotional Poetry
Recitations
Drama
Bible Plays
Sketches
Nativity Plays
Passiontide Plays
Easter Plays
Demonstrations
Resource Books
Assembly Material
Songs & Musicals
Children's Addresses
Prayers & Graces
Daily Readings
Books for Speakers
Activity Books
Quizzes
Puzzles
Painting Books
Daily Readings
Church Stationery
Notice Books
Cradle Rolls
Hymn Board Numbers

Please send a S.A.E. (approx 9" x 6") for the current catalogue or consult your local Christian Bookshop who should stock or be able to order our titles.